THE $\mathcal{A}$RT OF TENNIS

1874-1940

THE ART OF TENNIS

1874-1940

*Timeless, enchanting illustrations and narrative
of tennis' formative years*

GARY H. SCHWARTZ

MAGAZINE COVERS AND ILLUSTRATIONS
PICTURE POSTCARDS
ADVERTISING ILLUSTRATIONS

WOOD RIVER PUBLISHING
TIBURON, CALIFORNIA

The Art of Tennis

1874-1940

Copyright ©1990

by

Gary H. Schwartz

Wood River Publishing
680 Hawthorne Drive
Tiburon, CA 94920

First Edition November 1990

Design: Gabrielle Disario
Editing: Lee Berman
Copy Photography: Martin Zeitman
Printing: Times Offset, Singapore

Library of Congress Cataloging in Publication Data

ISBN: 0-9623000-4-7
CIP: 90-071173

TABLE OF CONTENTS

INTRODUCTION

"If this game is tolerated, play it in a quiet and gentlemanly manner."

Early description of tennis, Petrarch (1304-74)

*A*rtists, illustrators and photographers of the past have left behind a wonderful visual world of graphic material depicting the evolution of tennis. What better way to appreciate the rise of tennis to its eminent position in worldwide sports than by looking at the vehicles that originally represented the sport to the public: the magazine, the picture postcard and popular advertising.

The era of modern tennis began in England in 1874 with the patenting of the first packaged kit with instructions for playing the new game of lawn tennis by Major Walter Wingfield. Beginning with this period the art selections produced in this volume portray the infancy and growth not only of modern tennis but also of graphic illustration throughout the world. The result is a visual record of human ideas and social movements, as well as significant historical moments in the evolution of tennis as a sport. These works vividly highlight social, cultural and commercial fads and trends from the time of Major Wingfield to the onset of World War II in 1940, which marked the end of tennis' formative years. Of further interest is the delightful discovery that magazine covers, postcards and advertisements during this period were designed with such imagination and beauty.

Prior to the 1880s, when tennis began its period of dramatic growth in Great Britain and the United States, few working class people had the time or resources for outdoor amusement. Other sports, such as cricket, archery and polo were introduced in the United States before 1875, but were slow to gain a following in part due to a general American suspicion of any games imported from Britain.

Yet another factor affected tennis' slow initial acceptance. The public in many of the nations of the world were primarily sports spectators, not participants. Horse racing and prizefighting were constantly in the papers and in the United States baseball was on the rise. One exception was the rising popularity of cycling, but only for men. Most women in skirts could not expect to comfortably mount the high-wheel bicycle.

In fact, up until the 1880s no one popular activity had really emerged as a vehicle for mass recreation. That all changed in the decade of the 1880s with a dramatic rise in interest in tennis in the United States and much of the world. At the same time, popular exposure of the sport in magazines, advertising and picture postcards finally showed the unenlightened what fun it could be to volley a ball in the great outdoors.

In the early 1800s the sport of tennis and the art of graphic illustration were highly specialized and not yet generally accessible to the public. As the cost of reproducing illustrations decreased, however, more and more magazine, postcard and advertising art relating to tennis was offered to the growing middle class. Thus the growth of the sport paralleled its increasing popularity in the visual media.

New worlds were opened to people who discovered tennis through printed images.

Each visual resource played an important part in the public's perception of tennis and helped pique their interest. The sport began a growth spurt from a modest few thousand players to a sport that boasts perhaps 70 million avid participants today.

Tennis' formative years culminated in 1940, with the second World War. With the onset of war, international competition was suspended. At the same time, key technological advances in equipment began to appear. Coinciding with these developments were changes in the popular coverage of tennis through magazine illustrations, advertisements and picture postcards. Increasingly, photojournalism was to replace the work of magazine, advertising and postcard illustrators.

The post-World War II era marks the emergence of tennis as a big business. This growing commercial success has made tennis more accessible to the public than ever before. With more courts, better equipment and improved techniques more players daily are turning this sport of kings into the sport of millions.

The graphic works in this compilation show the cultural, social and commercial roles of the sport from 1874 to 1940, including changes in clothing, equipment, technique and public perceptions.

Many of the pictures in this volume depict tennis in an insightful, sensitive manner at a time when it was largely an elite, amateur pastime. The public tended to associate tennis with romance, leisure and fashion. Men and women alike had to be properly dressed for the occasion. For early women tennis players this involved an impractical ground-length wool dress with ornamental sleeves, high neck and cinched waist, worn with an elaborate hat; for men, fanciful tweeds, a straw boater hat and a fine tie.

Some of the graphics include touches of romance and sensuality. We encounter an idealized woman holding her racket, as though she was on the courts nearly every day, with perfect hair, wearing a glorious dress and, of course, a fashionable sun hat.

Viewing these illustrations also shows us that the same indomitable spirit that inspired the early tennis pioneers still characterizes the tennis player of today. The thrill and exhilaration of people participating in the sport of tennis certainly has not changed, although the style of the visual portrayal has evolved considerably.

Modern tennis is now well into its second century. The images contained in this volume are a large part of the history of tennis itself and paint a vivid picture of tennis' early years, 1874 to 1940.

Imagine now what it would be like to be among the first pioneers to roll out the net from your lawn tennis kit on the lush grassy estate of your friends, and volley the newly introduced rubber tennis ball towards your waiting partner. See yourself in front of a jazzy new automobile at a world class tennis club. Feel the sun, the challenge, and the excitement as you serve up a new adventure in sport...and in art.

HISTORY OF TENNIS

"If you know how to return my shots with a speedy left hand, I am yours."

Roman poet, Marcus Valerius Martialis (A.D. c.40-c.104)

Two players using gloves to protect their hands. The low sloping roof around the court was to become an important element of royal tennis. 14th century.

Three men playing court tennis, an indoor game, using string instead of a net. 1659.

Jeu de paume *being played out-of-doors. c.1789.*

*O*f all of mankind's inventions, the one that has given the greatest pleasure has been the ball. It is so wonderfully versatile that it is unsurpassed in the endless hours of enjoyment it brings to old and young alike.

Physically the ball can be dealt with in four ways. It can be thrown, caught, kicked and hit. It can also be produced in different sizes and shapes. Over time, a multitude of games have developed from various types of balls. The evolution of these different games is not always clearly documented, and this uncertainty applies to the origins of the game of tennis and to the people who first gave it to the world.

It is known that the early Greeks and Romans had games that were early precursors of tennis. References to these early variations occur in Greek and Roman literature and we can see some of them portrayed on Greek vases and early Roman coins.

The origin of tennis ultimately goes back to ancient times. There were many early games with balls and rackets. Primitive players first batted various types of balls with their hands, then later used protective gloves, which led to various extensions, including rackets.

Lawn tennis, as played during the past century, was derived from the ancient game of *real*, or *royal*, tennis. Real tennis appeared in Europe at the end of the Middle Ages, establishing standardization of rules and equipment, and this game is easily recognizable as an early precursor of the sport we now call tennis. It became a great fashion with sixteenth, seventeenth and eighteenth century noblemen, but after the French Revolution was virtually extinct.

Origin of Tennis Terminology

There has been much speculation as to why the game ever came to be called tennis. There is little doubt that tennis as we know it was originally a French game. The earliest known references to it occur in French manuscripts in the twelfth century. In France, the game was always known as *jeu de paume*, "the game of the palm," and it continues to be so called today. It has been suggested that early French players began a contest with the shout *tenez!*, that is, *play!*.

The method of scoring by fifteens is medieval in origin, with forty arising as an abbreviation of the original forty-five. The whole game was worth sixty points and was divided into four equal stages worth fifteen points each, as in squash. The number sixty had a special significance in medieval numerology — to begin with, there were sixty degrees in the segment of a circle, sixty minutes in an hour, sixty seconds in a minute, and so on. Deuce is simply a corruption of the French *à deux*, indicating that one player had to win two consecutive points for the game.

The use of the word *love* to mean no score has prompted a fair amount of fanciful speculation. It is probable that the expression "love" in tennis derives from early uses of the word to express the idea of nothing, as in such phrases as *a labor of love* and *neither for love nor money*.

Use of the word *service* to mark the opening stroke of each point is almost certainly derived from the fact that in the early days of tennis the ball was set in motion by a servant. Henry VIII (1509-47) employed a servant for this purpose, and in those days there was clearly no intention of winning a point by service; it was just a convenient way of starting a rally, a duty best performed by a lackey.

The Romans gave us the first words for *racket*. Its root is the Latin *reticulum* (small rete or "net"). From there it became *rachetta*, then racket.

Early Tennis in France

Real, or royal, tennis surfaced in France in the thirteenth century. It was first enjoyed in monastery courtyards, and it grew so popular that in 1245, the archbishop of Rouen prohibited priests from playing because they were ignoring their contemplative duties. Royalty quickly adopted the game, and *jeu de paume* became a favorite pastime of the French and English monarchy. Real tennis was distinguished by its galleries, the nature of the court, a convention called the *chase*, and its distinctive types of racket and balls.

Real tennis courts had gallery *roofs* jutting out around three of four sides, and points were won according to how the ball was hit into and through the galleries. The strange design of the hard-surfaced court is like the monastery cloisters where the game was first played. Today lawn tennis, the descendant of real tennis, is played on a rectangular court laid out on a grass surface. Play is within marked boundaries, and not played off of walls as in the original real tennis.

Apart from the obvious differences between lawn tennis and real tennis courts, the most striking difference between the two games lies in the occurrence in real tennis of the *chase*. The system of chases requires a *marker*, usually a professional, who stands at one end of the net. His task, beyond acting as umpire and keeping the score, is to *mark* the chases, that is to determine the point at which the ball strikes the

Short-handled rackets appear in this title page of the earliest extant set of rules for the game of tennis. 1632.

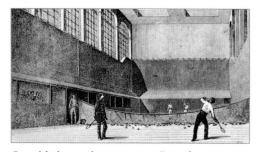

One of the last royal tennis courts in Paris, the Passage Cendrier, torn down in 1861.

floor on its second bounce. In lawn tennis, when a ball bounces twice, it is *dead* and the player on that side of the net loses the point. Not so in real tennis; instead, the ball makes a *chase* at the point of its second bounce, or if it enters one of the galleries, with its netted openings down one side of the court.

In either case, the marker records the position of the ball using a series of parallel lines marked out at the ends of the court. The player's objective is to place the second bounce as close as possible to the opponent's back wall. The marker keeps a record of the best chase of each player during the course of the game. In order to win a match, once a player has scored forty, he or she must also win the chase. The players take turns hitting the ball toward the back wall, winning points for the better chase. A player who has lagged in score due to an opponent's better agility can now come from behind to win the match by displaying superior skill at the chase.

Tennis first became a royal game in the reign of King Louis X of France (1314-16), who is said to have died of a chill contracted by drinking a beaker of cold water immediately after an energetic game of tennis. In those early days much betting took place on the outcome of a match. There is a story that a Duke of Burgundy twice pledged his doublet for a tennis debt, making him perhaps the first man ever to lose his shirt at the game.

Louis XI (1461-83) took a keen interest in tennis and in 1480 standardized the tennis ball. His son, Charles VIII (1483-98), became the second French king to lose his life as a result of tennis, when he struck his head on the lintel of the door leading to his court and subsequently died.

The golden age of real tennis in France took place in the sixteenth century. Francois I (1515-47) set the example, which was followed with enthusiasm by his courtiers and by common people all over France. He built courts wherever he went, including a covered court at the Louvre and an open court at Fontainebleau; he even included a tennis court on board his 2,000-ton, four-masted man-of-war, *La Grande Francoise*, built to outclass King Henry VIII of England's *Great Harry*.

The French Revolution put a stop to the royal game. But not before a tennis court had achieved immortal historical fame — the court at Versailles, scene of the famous "tennis-court oath." The Third Estate, locked out of the normal meeting place of the States-General by order of the King, met on June 20, 1789 on the tennis courts and vowed not to disband until France had a constitution. This dramatic beginning of the French Revolution is commemorated by a museum at the location of the court, dedicated to the onset of the Revolution.

Early tennis in Venice painted by Gabriele Bella. 16th century.

The future King Charles IX at age two. 1552.

James, Duke of York (later King James II). 1641.

The Spread of Tennis

Following its initial rise in popularity with French nobility, tennis spread from France throughout Europe. In England, the earliest mention of the game occurs in statutes forbidding it and encouraging the practice of more war-like skills such as archery. But such restraints did not apply to the King himself and it seems likely that Henry V (1413-22) was at least familiar with the game when he received a gift of tennis balls from the French Dauphin. In Shakespeare's play King Henry replies:

> *When we have matched our rackets to these balls,*
> *We will, in France, by God's grace, play a set,*
> *Shall strike his father's crown into the hazzard.*
> *Tell him, he hath made a match with such a wrangler,*
> *That all the courts in France will be disturbed*
> *With chases.*

As in France, the sixteenth century saw the establishment of tennis as the game of kings in England. Henry VIII (1509-47) was a very keen player and built a court at his Hampton Court palace, which is still used by tennis enthusiasts today.

Tennis was by no means confined to France and Britain. It was known in Spain from its early days and was played by Henry I (1214-17), King of Castile, who, like Louis X of France, is said to have died from drinking cold water immediately after an energetic game.

Early tennis was played in Italy, Holland, Switzerland, Sweden, the German states and throughout the Austro-Hungarian Empire, as well as in St. Petersburg (now Leningrad). A form of tennis also spread to the New World in the middle of the seventeenth century with a variation of the game played in New York.

Tennis went through a major decline during the eighteenth century, when the French Revolution and the Napoleonic wars wiped it out in France and most of Europe. At the same time, in England the game had lost its royal champion.

Fortunately, a significant revival took place in the nineteenth century in England with the rise of tennis under the stimulus of Victorian prosperity. Courts were built at many famous country houses. There was even a revival of royal interest in tennis when the Prince of Wales, later King Edward VII, played at Oxford in 1859.

Clubs that provided tennis for their members came into existence at this time, which helped spread the sport to other English-speaking countries. In 1874 a club, still in operation today, was opened in Tasmania, Australia. Tennis clubs also appeared around this time in Canada, France, Italy, Germany and other countries.

French painting of a distinguished tennis player. 18th century.

Why after so many centuries of real tennis did a new version of the game called *lawn tennis* suddenly appear in the 1870s and gain worldwide acceptance? On many occasions tennis enthusiasts had attempted to translate the earlier indoor game into an open-air sport, but all attempts failed for want of a suitable ball. The refinement of rubber was a crucial factor in the development of lawn tennis. The ball had to be soft enough not to damage the grass yet have the liveliness imparted to rubber, by vulcanization, a process only introduced in 1839. Another important factor was the portability of lawn tennis paraphernalia. All one needed was a flat grass surface, rather than the elaborate and expensive permanent courts of real tennis.

Other important contributions of nineteenth-century industry were the wealth that created a new leisure class and the railroads that carried its members to their country estates. Lawn tennis courts could be fashioned with ease on the lush, rolling grounds of the wealthy. The ability to entertain on one's own estate was certainly preferable to having to play on distant courts.

Lawn tennis soon acquired an upper-class stamp from the long tradition of real tennis as a sport of royalty and through certain characteristics of the game itself: it is limited to two or four people and is played on courts that take up considerable space and require expensive maintenance.

Arthur Balfour, British statesman and author of the Balfour Declaration, a chief basis for Israel's claim of sovereignty, is credited with having coined the name *lawn tennis*. Actual lawn-surface courts were superseded by derivative turf surfaces of various types. In most countries clay quickly was adopted as the logical surface for tennis. Concrete and other hard courts also were built, providing a quicker bounce for the ball. In addition, researchers have developed a range of new plastic materials that promise to make all natural surfaces obsolete.

The magnificent old game of real tennis is still regularly played by a small band of enthusiasts. The older game retains its charm, and its unique feature, the chase, gives encouragement to the less agile player. But tennis as a modern sport owes its growth to the invention and spread of lawn tennis with its advanced derivative surfaces.

The Birth and Spread of Lawn Tennis

Two men merit recognition as the founders of lawn tennis, Major Harry Gem, English solicitor and Clerk to the Birmingham Magistrates, and Major Walter Clopton Wingfield, member of England's Honourable Corps of Gentlemen-at-Arms at the court of Queen Victoria.

In 1858 Major Gem and Mr. J.B. Perera marked out a lawn in Edgbaston, England as a tennis court. While many of the accessories of real tennis were discarded, the game was clearly a variety of previous

Major Walter Clopton Wingfield at the age of forty, posing with one of the rackets sold by his representatives for a pound sterling each. 1870s.

Sketch drawn by Harry Gem, president and founder of the first Lawn Tennis Club in the world, the Leamington, England. Gem is about to hit the ball. His friend, G.B. Pereira plays at his side. 1872.

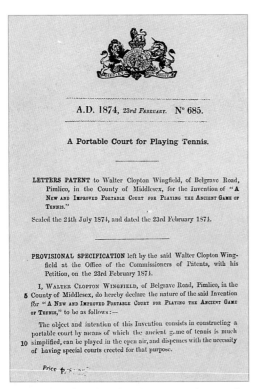

A.D. 1874, 23rd FEBRUARY. N° 685.

A Portable Court for Playing Tennis.

LETTERS PATENT to Walter Clopton Wingfield, of Belgrave Road, Pimlico, in the County of Middlesex, for the Invention of "A NEW AND IMPROVED PORTABLE COURT FOR PLAYING THE ANCIENT GAME OF TENNIS."

Sealed the 24th July 1874, and dated the 23rd February 1874.

PROVISIONAL SPECIFICATION left by the said Walter Clopton Wingfield at the Office of the Commissioners of Patents, with his Petition, on the 23rd February 1874.

I, WALTER CLOPTON WINGFIELD, of Belgrave Road, Pimlico, in the County of Middlesex, do hereby declare the nature of the said Invention for "A NEW AND IMPROVED PORTABLE COURT FOR PLAYING THE ANCIENT GAME OF TENNIS," to be as follows:—

The object and intention of this Invention consists in constructing a portable court by means of which the ancient game of tennis is much simplified, can be played in the open air, and dispenses with the necessity of having special courts erected for that purpose.

Price 5d.

Wingfield's request for a patent for "a new and improved portable court for playing the ancient game of tennis."

The first known photograph of lawn tennis, at Leamington, England. 1874.

The scene at the very first Wimbledon Championships. 1877.

tennis games. For twelve years the game thrived on Edgbaston turf until 1870 when a move was made to Leamington. The Leamington Lawn Tennis Club, the world's first club devoted exclusively to lawn tennis, was founded in 1872 with Major Gem as president.

Major Gem and his friends were not unique in adapting tennis as a lawn game. Attempts were made to play tennis outdoors in Elizabethan times. But the prime honor as founder of lawn tennis has for long been accorded to Major Walter Wingfield, whose bust adorns the entrance hall of the Lawn Tennis Association headquarters in London.

The first record of Major Wingfield playing his version of lawn tennis was at Lansdowne House in London in 1869 with a net two feet high. In February 1874 he designed a packaged tennis kit and applied for a patent for his "Portable Court for Playing Tennis." The next month he issued the first edition of his booklet *Sphairistike* which explained the game, and which he began packing in his tennis kits. The use of this Greek word, meaning "ball game," was possible only in an age when all gentlemen were presumed to have acquaintance with the classics. The name was soon contracted to "Sticky" and that in turn abandoned to the use of the alternative description "Lawn Tennis." The patent received provisional protection for three years but was not extended further. Wingfield continued to sell his sets of tennis paraphernalia, which attained immediate popularity, particularly among the upper levels of society.

The original court on the lawn had an hourglass figure, narrower at the net than at the base lines. The balls were uncovered hollow rubber. The net was about four feet high in the center and five feet at each of the two posts. This original lawn tennis court was a derivative of previously designed tennis and badminton courts.

It was not long before lawn tennis began to replace croquet as a summer pastime. Manufacturers began to produce their own versions of tennis sets. There were soon about as many codes of rules as there were players.

In 1875 significant events took place in London which had a momentous influence on the development of tennis. From a pastime it was transformed into a sport.

The All England Croquet Club, founded in 1869, had failed to thrive. Its four acres near Worple Road in the London suburb of Wimbledon underwent continual rises in rent payments, and it became increasingly difficult for the club to make ends meet.

As a result, in 1875 when Mr. Henry Jones, one of the club's founders, suggested lawn tennis as an added attraction, the idea was approved. The new game prospered, so much so that by 1877 the name was changed to the All England Croquet and Lawn Tennis Club. However, the club had still not improved its financial position sufficiently to cover its rising overhead. Henry Jones proposed a lawn tennis tournament for all comers. J.H. Walsh, editor of *The Field*, liked the idea and persuaded his proprietors to support it. *The Field* offered a silver challenge cup valued at twenty-five guineas. The first Wimbledon Championship was born.

A committee was appointed to draw up a set of rules which would end the confusions which had arisen about scoring, the size of the net and the court. Some modifications were made in later years, but their basic formula stood the test of time and play.

The early years were full of technical and strategic experiments. The first tournament at Wimbledon in 1877 boasted twenty-two participants and was viewed by 200 spectators. Afterwards there was some controversy about the way matches had been dominated by service, and some critics wanted to ban the overhand service. They were mainly supporters of real tennis and argued to no avail that the new game should be an exercise in the art of rallying.

By 1896 the Wimbledon tournament was no longer reserved for the British. The Americans had entered and the rest of the world followed: by 1905 the number of entries was seventy-one, and the countries represented included the United States, Australia, Belgium, Denmark, New Zealand, Sweden and South Africa.

The 1920s and 1930s saw tremendous growth of the sport of tennis around the world. In 1938 Don Budge won the Big Slam and Helen Wills Moody celebrated her eighth victory at Wimbledon. In 1939 three Wimbledon titles were awarded to both Bobbie Riggs and Alice Marble. With the onset of World War II, the classic early growth era of tennis had come to an end.

The post-World War II generation brought a great transformation to the sport. Tennis was now a popular avocation, with technical improvements making it far more sophisticated. Tennis finally made its entrance into the modern age. The 1950s saw the rise of Jack Kramer's tremendous popularity. Postwar affluence and television all combined to move tennis into the class of big-money professional sports and to attract millions of new followers. Tennis became accessible to the vast middle class, and television was ready and eager to give people massive doses of the sport. Tennis had become big business.

While the popular acceptance of the sport was originally that of lawn tennis, today the sport is played on clay, cement, wood and plastic courts, as well as on grass in nearly every country of the world.

Tennis in the United States

Tennis arrived in the United States via New York harbor in 1874, when Mary Ewing Outerbridge of Staten Island landed from Bermuda with a package containing paraphernalia so unusual that it was held up by customs before she could recover it a few weeks later. She had discovered tennis while visiting her brother, Sir Joseph

The fifth round of the All-Comers Match at Wimbledon. Renshaw versus Lawford. 1881.

Wingfield's new game was set up on board the steamship Canima *while he was on the way to New York with Mary Outerbridge. 1874.*

Mixed doubles at Cleremont, Bermuda, then the home of Sir Brownlow and Lady Grey. The tennis court was the first in the western hemisphere, before Major Wingfield's patent on the game. 1873.

The Staten Island Cricket Club courts, six years after the Outerbridges first played there.

The first National Lawn Tennis Tournament in Staten Island, New York. 1880.

The inner court of the Newport Casino.

Outerbridge, on the Bermuda estate of Sir Brownlow Gray, and she brought back a net, rackets and balls with a set of instructions.

This game bore little resemblance to the one banned by Peter Stuyvesant, the Dutch governor of New Amsterdam, on October 15, 1659. This act was the first official recognition that a game called tennis was being played in the territory that was to become New York. The ban was effective. No one had the slightest idea what Miss Outerbridge's game was all about, and even her own knowledge was rudimentary.

Miss Outerbridge got permission to set up a court on a corner of the Staten Island Cricket and Baseball Club grounds, and it was not long before other lawn courts made their appearance in the East. In the West the first concrete courts were installed in Santa Monica, California, in 1879.

The first men's U.S. national championships were held in August 1881 at the Newport Casino in Rhode Island, an elegant new club built out of spite by James Gordon Bennett, the flamboyant publisher of the New York *Herald*. On a bet, a guest of his named Captain Candy, a member of the visiting British polo team, had ridden a horse into the ultra-exclusive men's club called the Reading Room, and his guest's privileges were promptly revoked. The stuffiness of the Reading Room was taken as a personal affront by Bennett, who thought Newport needed a new, lively social center.

The Casino, designed by Charles McKim and Stanford White, brought European ideas of a social center to America for the first time. There was a dance twice weekly in the ballroom, concerts on an open bandstand, and a great field of lush lawn-tennis courts and a grandstand overlooking the courts where America's nationals were played for thirty-four successive years.

In New York during the 1880s tennis was making its appearance in Central Park. Informal grass courts gave way to smoother clay courts with fences, but there were not enough of them for the hundreds of New Yorkers eager to play. Clubs soon sprung up in the suburbs.

Tennis clubs, at least at their inception, were started because of the insufficiency of public courts. Local governments were not prepared to meet the recreational demands of tennis players when the game first appeared. Basketball, baseball, football, track and swimming were publicly subsidized because of the larger numbers served by the facilities. One tennis court used for twelve hours for doubles, bringing in new players hourly, can serve only forty-eight people. Only golf is more cost-intensive than tennis.

The United States National Lawn Tennis Association (USLTA) was organized in 1881 to establish the official rules of play, scoring, the height of the net, the distance of the service line from the net, and the size of the ball. With thirty-four clubs represented, the first official championship was conducted that year at the newly constructed Newport Casino in Rhode Island.

The United States Lawn Tennis Association Championships, singles and doubles, were held at the Newport Casino from their inception in 1881 until 1914. However, the West Side Tennis Club in New York was not pleased with the Newport Casino. They felt the crowd came there not to watch tennis but to be seen. The nationals were as much a fashion show as a tennis tournament. Compared to Wimbledon, Newport was not a serious center of tennis. Many members of the West Side Tennis Club were dismayed by the atmosphere when they played in the championships or went up to watch them.

The West Side members bid to move the nationals out of Newport and to New York's new grass courts. Here, at a serious tennis center, they asserted, the crowds would be true tennis fans rather than beautiful matrons showing off their huge hats and new egret feathers. To prove this the club was invited in 1911 to stage the Davis Cup matches with Great Britain. Public interest was such that 3,000 people a day came to the wooden stands at the West Side Courts, confirming that good tennis could draw well in New York.

With the completion in 1924 of the new West Side Tennis Club stadium in Forest Hills, New York, the Championships found a permanent home, where they have been held ever since.

The USLTA Women's Singles Championships began in 1887 at the Chestnut Hill Lawn Tennis Club on the grass courts of the Philadelphia Cricket Club, where they remained through 1920. Since 1921 the Championship has been held at the West Side Tennis Club, Forest Hills, New York.

Lawn tennis practice at the Seventh Regiment Armory, New York. 1881.

The first Ladies Open Lawn Tennis Tournament, Staten Island, New York. 1883.

Tennis Around the World

The first international seeds of tennis were sown from the very beginning. When Major Gem marked out his court in Edgbaston, England, he did so with a Portuguese gentleman named Mr. Perera. By the early 1880s the game had spread around the world. It was played in Panama in 1878. In 1881 there was a tournament in Durban, South Africa, where championships date to 1891.

Europe

British players introduced the game to France, in particular to resorts in the Riviera and at Dinard and Le Touquet. The first club in France was the Decimal Club, founded in Paris in 1877. The German championships began in 1893. Belgium began its national championships in 1895, Switzerland in 1898. A European championship, staged at different venues in different countries, was started in 1899 and continued until after World War I. When the first of the modern Olympics was held in Athens in 1896, lawn tennis was one of its sports.

Japan

Tennis was formally introduced into Japan in 1880 by George Adams Leland, an American who had been invited by the Japanese government to be an instructor at the Training Institute for Physical Education Teachers. Leland taught his students to play with rackets and balls he had brought from the United States. The new game was received with great interest, but since equipment had to be imported it was quite expensive.

Graduates of the Training Institute were employed at schools throughout Japan, and it was not long before tennis spread widely. In 1887 the two tennis courts in the compounds of the British Legation in Tokyo were made available for an international group of tennis enthusiasts sponsored by the British Minister. The Japanese government was impressed by these efforts and gave a grant of grounds in the heart of Tokyo for tennis courts. This led to the founding of the most active and distinguished international tennis club in Japan, which is now the Tokyo Lawn Tennis Club, formally established after the turn of the century.

Australia and New Zealand

The first Australian lawn tennis championship tournament took place in Melbourne in 1880, followed by the State Championship held by the Sydney Lawn Tennis Club at the Sydney Cricket Ground in New South Wales in 1885. Queensland sponsored a championship tournament in 1890, South Australia in 1890, Tasmania in 1893 and Western Australia in 1895. During this period, until the first World War, many Australians considered tennis to be a social game, not to be compared as a sport with the more rugged team games. After the war, however, for many Australians tennis became almost a religion.

The first lawn tennis club in New Zealand is believed to have been formed as early as 1875. The first national championships were staged eleven years later in 1886.

The first Australian national championships had to wait for the creation of Australia as a nation in 1905. Australia, as a tennis nation, has figured prominently on the international scene since 1907, when the first foreigner to win the title at Wimbledon, Norman Brookes, was an Australian. Since that time, nineteen Australian men and four Australian women have won the Wimbledon title. The early years of the Davis Cup, with only one exception from 1907 to 1914, were dominated by the team from Australia and New Zealand, on five occasions represented by Brookes and New Zealand's Tony Wilding.

Canada

Not long after the Canadian Confederation was proclaimed in 1867, interest in the game of lawn tennis began to spread and develop. The Toronto Lawn Tennis Club was formed before what is believed to

Mixed doubles at the Club de Dinard, a resort where lawn tennis was popular in its early days. c. 1890.

King Gustav V of Sweden, second from the left, and Prince Chichibu, son of the Emperor of Japan (third from left), at Nice, France. 1926.

be Canada's first officially recorded tennis tournament, played in 1878. Interest in tennis mushroomed throughout Canada during the years that followed.

Canada entered worldwide competition for the first time in 1913, in the Davis Cup tournament, which the team lost to the United States in the finals.

Tennis Equipment

The Tennis Ball

The original tennis ball was made from sheepskin and filled with sawdust, sand or wool. It did not bounce on grass at all. King Louis XI of France decreed in 1480 that balls should be covered with good leather (usually sheepskin) and filled with good hair or wool stuffing, and that the filling should not be adulterated, as had often been the practice, by using old rags or bran. In the early years the ball was struck with the hand and consequently a rigid specification for the ball was unnecessary.

In England, tennis balls were made by the Ironmongers' Company for their own company tennis court. They soon found it profitable to make them for other London players. The right was jealously guarded as shown by a petition to Edward IV in about 1470, praying that the king prohibit the import of *tenys balles*.

The tightly packed balls of real tennis bounced well enough on hard stone floors but not at all on grass. When Major Harry Gem formed the first lawn tennis club in Leamington, England in 1872, he specified that the club would use only the newly developed rubber balls, which quickly replaced real tennis balls on the courts.

Latex (rubber) comes from the stems of rubber trees. It was not until the nineteenth century that rubber-tree seeds were brought to Europe and grown commercially. Then as now rubber was vulcanized (treated with sulphur at high temperatures) to make it stronger and more elastic. The hollow ball is formed from two halves bonded together. Because the plain rubber ball proved to be rather slippery in wet conditions, a flannel covering was soon invented.

By the time of the first Wimbledon championships in 1877, specifications for the tennis ball had been established. The cloth cover which had been sewn at the seam was first cemented in 1924, and this procedure soon became the new standard. In about 1931 the pressure inside the ball was increased. The result was a lively ball with remarkably similar specifications to the tennis balls in use today.

The Tennis Racket

The Italians are thought to have been the first to protect the hand with a glove when playing precursors to real tennis. The glove not only protected the palm but also afforded greater power for driving the

Norman Brookes, in his familiar cloth cap, was Australia's great hope in the 1914 Davis Cup matches at Forest Hills.

The Canadian Lawn Tennis Tournament in Toronto. 1881.

Examples of early tennis balls.

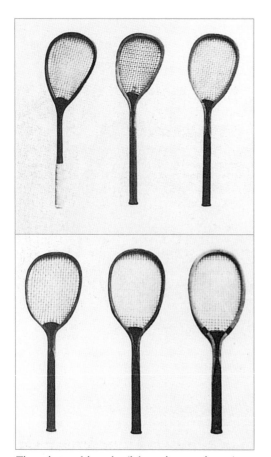

The evolution of the racket (left to right, top to bottom): 1874, 1875, 1878, 1879, 1880 and 1908.

ball. The next logical step was the idea of stretching an elastic network of catgut strings across the glove, and then of affixing a handle to the apparatus.

This racket, or *battoir*, consisted of little more than a strengthened glove with a short handle. The battoir soon developed into a wooden frame over which a parchment was stretched. From this experiment, designers learned that the catgut originally fastened to a glove could be used to better effect if strung on a wooden frame.

Playing with the hand and with a racket were accepted as alternative methods for many years until finally, with various improvements, the racket proved more efficient.

When Major Harry Gem played the first organized game of lawn tennis in 1872, players used classic (real) tennis rackets. Special lawn-tennis rackets were not introduced until 1874 when Major Walter Wingfield started to market his "Sphairistike or Lawn Tennis." His rackets had long handles and a slightly smaller head. Major Wingfield's rules placed no restriction on the size or shape of the racket and before long all kinds were produced with the intention, according to the advertisements, of aiding the player.

Rackets came in a great variety of styles, including widely spaced, diagonally strung strings, knotted gut and even a parchment center. A racket with a curved handle (known as a "bent" racket) was sold in the United States; its advantage, according to its creators, was that the head always pointed back towards the court to which the ball should be played. Other rackets had mercury in the hollow handle to transfer the weight, when a shot was played, from the handle to the head.

Tennis Fashion

The first women to play tennis were English and Irish. Since the social circumstances attending the birth of lawn tennis led people to view it as a royal game, it naturally evolved as a sport adopted by the leisured classes, for whom etiquette in both behavior and appearance was all important.

Without special rules or precedents the first women players wore what they would have chosen for a garden party: an elaborately flounced ground-length dress with ornamented sleeves, high neck and cinched waist, worn over a bustle, corset, petticoats and long drawers complemented by an elaborate hat. Their first concession to practicality was to adopt flat rubber-soled shoes, invariably black so they would not be visibly soiled by the grass.

Tennis costumes varied little from party clothes until increasing movement about the courts made perspiration a problem. At that time it was unthinkable for a lady to be seen perspiring, and with the beginning of tournament, or public play in 1879, a strong case for all-white dress was put forward.

Fashions of the time were displayed by actress Louise Grudy, as she appeared in The Night Boat. *c.1915.*

Women were first admitted to Wimbledon in 1884, wearing the all-white costume of the day. By the turn of the century the bustle had disappeared, colored ribbon bands with brooch fastenings were replacing collars, and women were seen outdoors for the first time without hats.

In 1905 an American, May Sutton, the first Wimbledon champion from overseas (and thus unconstrained by British etiquette) caused widespread indignation by rolling back her sleeves from her wrists because she was "too hot." This was the first instance of a woman player putting performance before etiquette. In doing so, Miss Sutton created the first significant milestone in the progress of tennis fashion.

The arrival of the French player, Suzanne Lenglen, at the reopening of Wimbledon in 1919, influenced all future tennis fashion. Lenglen appeared in a flimsy, one-piece cotton frock. The skirt was pleated from the waist but it reached only to mid-calf. Moreover, it was worn without petticoats or corsets, and its short sleeves showed her bare elbows. The effect was staggering. She was described as "shocking" and spoken of as "indecent," but her all-conquering supremacy at the game coincided with the beginning of women's postwar liberation. Her daring exactly matched the mood of the hour, and in a short time she had an adoring following. Suzanne Lenglen gave lawn tennis an importance never previously known in sport and revolutionized the entire concept of women's dress, on and off the courts.

Helen Wills ruled the Centre Court at Wimbledon from 1927 to 1938, never varying her attire.

In 1932 Helen Jacobs offered tennis' next shocker when she played the ladies' singles final in what are now called Bermuda-length shorts. This new exposure led to culotte skirts, which bridged the gap between ever-shortening hemlines and prevailing concepts of modesty. The comfortable culotte skirt held its role in woman's tennis fashions up to the outbreak of World War II.

Competition

Tennis was clearly a competitive game from the very start. Though it was always a pleasure to hit a tennis ball about in the company of friends, the highest delight was in acquiring superior skill and becoming a better player.

The first recorded international match took place in 1883, when James Dwight and Richard Sears were chosen to represent the United States as a team at Wimbledon in July. They played against the famous British twins, William and Ernest Renshaw. After losing to the British, Dwight and Sears came back the next year and made it into the finals of the Wimbledon Championships. By 1889 E.G. Meers, one of the top ten male players in Britain, crossed the Atlantic to play in the official American championship. There was an increasing interchange of players thereafter, and the national rivalry in due course led to the inauguration of the Davis Cup competition in 1900.

Suzanne Lenglen's dress influenced all future tennis fashion. 1925.

Dr. James Dwight, dapper in his stiff collar and straw hat. c.1900.

The Davis Cup, more properly the International Lawn Tennis Championship, had its origins in Anglo-American rivalry which dates from the game's cradle days. As early as 1883 there was an international doubles at the All England Club, Wimbledon. The first official moves to promote the competition were made in 1897 when, following an invitation by the president of the U.S. Lawn Tennis Association, the Council of the British Lawn Tennis Association approved a resolution "that it is desirable in the interests of lawn tennis that a match be arranged between the United Kingdom and the United States."

It was not until 1900 that the Davis Cup, one of the greatest of international sporting events, began. By then the original concept had widened to include any nation which had a recognized Lawn Tennis Association. Dwight F. Davis of St. Louis donated the trophy, a massive silver punch bowl lined with gold and valued at a thousand dollars.

What began as a challenge match between the United States and Great Britain in 1900 quickly developed into a worldwide competition with Davis Cup teams from dozens of countries.

As a pastime, one of the social delights of early lawn tennis was the ability of men and women to play together. As an organized sport it cast women in a less important role, not only because of disparities in established social conventions but also because of the physical restriction of women's clothing. The overhead service did not become commonplace among women until after World War I.

The Irish pioneered championship lawn tennis for women in 1879, staging both a singles and mixed tournament, though not a women's doubles. Wimbledon involved women for the first time in 1884, though the event did not flourish until the turn of the century.

In the United States, the Philadelphia Cricket Club organized the first women's championship in 1887. The pioneers of women's lawn tennis were an extraordinary group of stalwarts. Not until 1902 was the women's singles in the U.S. Nationals reduced from a grueling best of five sets to the best of three.

The *Big Four* international tournaments encompass Wimbledon, the U.S. Nationals at Forest Hills, New York, the French Championships and the Australian Championships. Although the Australian and French Championships are linked with Wimbledon and the U.S. Nationals as part of the Big Four, they have never really measured up to their fellow tournaments.

The French event was first held in 1891 on red clay courts at Stade Roland Garros, outside Paris. Perhaps this is one reason for its semi-major status, since traditionally great championships must be won on grass, the original surface. Moreover the tournament is held in late spring, prior to Wimbledon, when many players have yet to get into top shape.

William (left) and Ernest Renshaw, the famous British twins. 1880s.

Geography is Australia's nemesis. Located at the bottom of the globe, half a world away from most thriving tennis centers, Australia was always considered an isolated tennis nation. With reversed seasons from the northern hemisphere, and because other countries were reluctant to send players so far, there was never a substantial overseas entry in the early Australian Championships. As a result, the Australians had their own national tournament largely to themselves, with only periodic threats from the outside. There were only three non-Australian men's singles champions prior to 1940, and only two women's.

The Great Players

Bill Tilden (U.S.A.) is truly one of the immortals in the sports world. Considered by many to the be greatest tennis player ever, Tilden had everything, including a cannonball service. He was invincible in the U.S. Championships for six consecutive years; he won Wimbledon at the age of 37 in 1930. His finest achievement was in taking thirteen successive singles in the Challenge Round of the Davis Cup between 1920 and 1926. Tilden furthermore matched his exceptional skill with a commanding personality. He was as intellectual as he was athletic and wrote both plays and books.

In 1922 Tilden had part of a finger removed but was able remarkably to adapt his grip. He became a professional in 1931 and was still playing great tennis up to his death in 1953.

Except for Suzanne Lenglen, France caused no big stir in international tennis until the mid-1920s, with the appearance of four players who came to be known as the "Four Musketeers." One of these players, Henri Cochet (France) stood out as a player of rare genius — his ability to half volley and always to take an exceptionally early ball enabled him to dispense with the normal demands of quick footwork. He looked lazy on the court, was unpredictable and sometimes had bad defeats, but he was none the less one of the greatest players of all time. Remarkably, Cochet defeated Tilden twice at Wimbledon and three times in Davis Cup play.

Jean-René Lacoste (France) was the supreme baseline player with a remarkable control of the ball and depth of stroke. No player was more calculating than Lacoste, who analyzed each opponent's game for its weaknesses and strong points. He was a master of the lob, with few equals. Lacoste's match with Tilden in the 1927 final of the U.S. Championship was a classic demonstration of two of the greatest players of all time. For nearly two hours the thirty-four year old Tilden attacked with drive, chop and slice, and with cannonball and twist serves. Tilden resorted to the volley as he rarely had before, brought all his cunning and courtcraft to bear, and fought with a courage that never wavered. Yet he could not win a set.

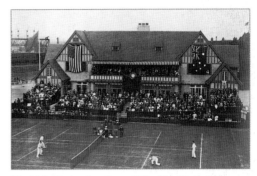

The U.S. Nationals at Forest Hills, New York. 1914.

Bill Tilden's name remains synonomous with excellence in every phase of tennis. He was a master of all the strokes and was tennis' first true professional.

Don Budge invented the Grand Slam by winning the nationals in Australia, France, England and the United States. 1938.

Jack Kramer: perhaps the greatest volley player ever.

That was Lacoste's second successive victory in the U.S. Championship, making him the first player from overseas to win the title twice. Lacoste's victory over Tilden in the 1927 Challenge Round was the key match that won the Davis Cup for France for the first time. He won Wimbledon in 1925 and 1928 and the French title in 1925, 1927 and 1929. Historians still argue about how great Lacoste might have been had not his failing health forced him to withdraw from tennis after 1929, at the age of only 25.

Fred Perry (Great Britain) broke the tradition that tennis champions were stuffy, upper crust and proper. Perry was a cocky, arrogant man who gained tremendous spectator loyalty as he vanquished the game's class distinctions. He won the U.S. Championships in 1934 and 1936, the French Championships in 1935 and the Australian Nationals in 1934. Perry became a true world champion when he won Wimbledon successively in 1934, 1935 and 1936.

Don Budge (U.S.A.) had a rolled backhand that changed the technique of the game, transforming what had been a defensive stroke into an attacking one. Probably no player of any time had a better return of service. Budge was the first player to win the Grand Slam when he took the four major championships in 1938. Many still debate whether Tilden or Budge was the greatest player of all time. Tilden wrote in the 1947 edition of his book, *My Story*, "For all-round consistency Donald Budge at the peak of his game was the finest of them all. I consider him the finest player 365 days a year that ever lived."

Jack Kramer (U.S.A.) was to become the outstanding player of the immediate post-World War II period. Kramer was a sterling competitor and incredible athlete with superb strokes. Kramer was a tall man who made full use of his height in a powerful service and overhead. He brought the volley into play without delay, going in on virtually every serve on fast surfaces and often on his return of service.

Suzanne Lenglen (France) was a legendary all-time great player with an unparalleled record of invincibility. In eight years of play (1919-26), until she became a professional, she was only once beaten in singles. During the 1921 U.S. Championships she became sick and retired after losing the first set in her opening match. Her ball control was impeccable and she leaped about the court like a ballerina. In winning the 1925 Wimbledon she lost only five games; in winning the French title in 1926 she lost only four. Lenglen's incomparable skill and magnetic personality helped transform lawn tennis into a major spectator sport. In at least five major tournaments she won every singles round 6-0, 6-0.

Helen Wills Moody (U.S.A.) was second only to Suzanne Lenglen in her record of invincibility and certainly one of the great all-time players. She won the Wimbledon singles eight times, a record in nine challenges, and in 1927-32 did not lose a set in singles anywhere. She paraded her superb driving skill without sign of emotion and was known as "Little Poker Face." Her estrangement from the American authorities made her a non-competitor in the U.S. Championships after 1933.

Alice Marble (U.S.A.) played lawn tennis more like a man than any other woman of her time. She volleyed incessantly, going in on her service, and also took the ball on the rise off the ground. Few women mastered the overhead smash or the American twist service as she did. Trim of figure, she moved quickly and gracefully, and, both in her appearance and her style of game, she was one of the most attractive women players of all time. Her game at its peak was a delight to watch.

Helen Jacobs (U.S.A.) won the U.S. Championships four years in a row, won the title at Wimbledon where she was runner-up five times (four times to Helen Wills Moody), and was one of the very few people to defeat the reigning champion, Wills Moody, in 1933. She was one of the best women volleyers of them all, with a strong overhead, and she had a backhand that stood like Gibraltar under the heaviest bombardment.

Conclusion

The popular game of tennis, as we know it today, has evolved from an elite pastime of royalty to a world-class competitive sport that boasts millions of participants and spectators internationally. The illustrations in this volume bring to light a period of popular cultural art that influenced changes in public perceptions of the sport. These years were exciting and dynamic in their visual presentations, as is the sport of tennis in its appeal to the millions who adore it.

Suzanne Lenglen, the greatest French star, leaps to hit an acrobatic overhand. 1913.

The arrival at Centre Court for the last Wimbledon match between Helen Wills (left) and Helen Jacobs. 1938.

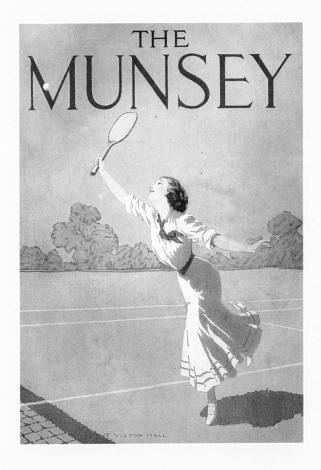

The Munsey. *T. Victor Hall. 1909.*

HISTORY OF MAGAZINE ILLUSTRATION

"A work of art cannot be satisfied with being a representation, it should be a presentation."

Jacques Reverdy French artist, twentieth century

$\mathcal{T}$he first magazines were published in France in 1665. Others soon followed around the world, and they were typical of the visually dry and textually dull publications that appeared during the first 200 years of magazine history. Most publishers did not realize the significance of visuals as tools to educate, shape opinions, entertain, and sell greater numbers of their magazines.

During the mid-nineteenth century the magazine began to change from an elitist publication to the main source of popular entertainment for the general public. Instead of speaking primarily to the well-educated upper classes, the magazine addressed a broad cross section of the population. Aided and inspired by the cultural and technical changes of the Industrial Revolution, the new, modern magazine enjoyed a dramatic rise in popularity in Europe, the United States and elsewhere. By 1890 it had begun its most colorful period.

Through the addition of illustrations the periodical achieved a new character and vitality in the Victorian Age. With the emergence of the magazine, art could be disseminated to substantial numbers of people for the first time in history.

Until that time all art forms had been relatively inaccessible to the general public, remaining in the hands of privileged friends and patrons of the artists or publicly displayed in faraway cities. The sport of tennis was likewise generally inaccessible up to this time. As the public's appreciation of art grew, the magazine proved to be an important stage upon which artists of all kinds could depict tennis in all its romantic glory.

The magazine cover, like the magazine itself, had been neglected as a decorative element in its early years. But with the increase in vivid dramatic illustrations came the discovery that the magazine cover had important powers to influence and amuse.

Great Britain took the early lead in producing illustrated periodicals during the nineteenth century. Publishers, as well as master engravers and artists, sensed the public's readiness to spend a shilling a copy to enjoy the latest illustrations, which were often eyewitness accounts of current events.

The first tennis cartoon published in Punch Magazine. *1876.*

There are two apparent reasons for the emergence of Great Britain as the early leader of illustrated periodicals and books: its efficient communications system for distribution of publications and its educated public to read them. However, other countries soon began to catch up with and eventually surpass Great Britain in the visual arts.

With the emergence of *Frank Leslie's Illustrated Weekly* and *Harper's Weekly*, the modern illustrated periodical was born in America. It took American marketing ingenuity to become the link that delivered the magazine into the hands of vast numbers of people.

The late nineteenth century was a time of great social change during which the traditional class structures were being eroded. Magazines were an important focus for people as they experienced a shifting of social values. Tennis was brought to light through accounts and illustrations of early visitors to England, Wales and elsewhere.

Perhaps the 1890s should have been called the *more decade*. The nineties brought more money, more leisure, education, sports and entertainment. As travelers discovered tennis, it followed that the sport of tennis would be extensively offered to the magazine public.

Production of magazines went through revolutionary changes during the late nineteenth century. Until that time, it was a difficult, time-consuming and costly task to produce the visuals accompanying magazine text. Publications would often share the $300 to $500 cost for a full page woodcut with other publishers. This prohibitive cost was reduced as technological changes made economies of scale possible. At the same time technological changes in tennis equipment led to economies of scale and reductions in cost.

A typical magazine illustration took three weeks to complete in the mid-nineteenth century. By 1872 the process of making an illustration from start to finish took one week. Ten years later it had been refined to two days, and by 1900 shortened to a few hours. Photoengraving came into use about this time, radically reducing the time and cost for producing magazine graphics. It reduced a long laborious process to a simple, mechanical one.

In addition to photography, the other important technical advancement for magazine illustrations was the color revolution. Color lithography enabled magazines to display beautiful works of art with a quality never dreamed possible by most people. The color revolution produced intensified public interest in prints, posters and magazine covers. As a result, important artists such as Will Bradley, Edward Penfield, Charles Dana Gibson and Maxfield Parrish were drawn to these media. Other famous illustrators included Harrison Fisher (The Fisher Girl), Howard Chandler Christy (The Christy Girls), Jessie Wilcox Smith (wide-eyed children), and Norman Rockwell (all-American scenes).

Suzanne Lenglen at fifteen years, shaking hands with Madame Broquedis. 1914.

The New Yorker. 1938.

Magazines used vivid illustrations to attract readers, showing the sport of tennis in all its picturesque beauty, depicting people from all walks of life enjoying the challenge and grace of the sport.

Looking at magazine covers, one can understand the important interaction between the magazine and fine art. Clearly, the magazine, and its cover in particular, comprised an important medium allowing many remarkable artists to test their artistic and experimental works in public. The cover also became a medium through which fine art was diffused into a commercial form more readily available to the masses.

During the early decades of the twentieth century, the magazine industry flourished. Since radio did not enter most households until the early 1920s, magazines enjoyed a captive market. There were fears, of course, that the popularity of radio would completely smother the magazine industry. Fortunately, it did not.

One of the keys to the success of magazine publishing was the increase in advertising, which helped lower the price of each magazine, which in turn, boosted circulation. Advertisers pumped large sums of money into the industry, as they discovered that the buying power of the rising middle class could best be tapped through magazines.

The biggest effect felt by the magazine industry in the 1930s was not that of the Depression or international political tension, but the publication in the United States of *Life* magazine in 1936. With ninety-six pages of photographs and only a minimum of text, *Life* brought photo-journalism into unprecedented importance, as the photographer took the magazine cover away from the illustrator.

This introduction of photographic accounts proved to be decisive. It signaled the beginning of the end of the period of predominance of magazine illustrations. But it was also decisive in bringing forth a new awareness and public enthusiasm for modern tennis.

Mid-Week Pictorial. *1928.*

The New Yorker. *1935.*

Lawn Tennis. The Illustrated London News. *1880.*

The ladies' lawn tennis tournament, Staten Island Cricket Club grounds.
Harper's Weekly. *C.D. Weldon. 1883.*

"*Two's company.*" Harper's Bazar. *J.N. Marble. 1888.*

The North Meadows, Central Park. Harper's Weekly. W.T. Smedley.
1889.

Tennis Costumes. Harper's Bazar. 1888.

The first day of the season. The Illustrated London News. *1891.*

"It is for you, Mr. Christopher," said Lucy. Harper's Bazar. *1882.*

Lawn Tennis in Prospect Park. Harper's Weekly. *T. de Thulstrup. 1885.*

The lawn tennis match at Prince's Club, England. The Graphic. 1883.

The championship lawn tennis match: Mr. Hartley winning the Wimbledon cup for the second time. The Illustrated London News. 1880.

The Saturday Evening Post. *Harrison Fisher*. 1901.

Lippincott's. *William L. Corqueville. 1895.*

"Play!" *C.W. Gibson. c.1900.*

They contested every point hotly. Scribner's. *Karl Anderson. 1904.*

Playing lawn tennis in Alexandria, Egypt.
The Graphic. *Reginald Cleaver. 1894.*

The Munsey. *Y. Wright. 1901.*

By-Play. Harrison Fisher. 1906.

The Ladies' Home Journal. *Henry Hutt. 1907.*

Skipped by the Light of the Moon. Dudley Hardy. 1900.

Woman's Home Companion. *Marion Powers. 1912.*

Collier's. *Arthur Mosgon. 1923.*

The Country Gentleman. *J. Knowles Hare. 1924.*

Illustrated Sunday Magazine. *Emerson. 1915.*

The People's Home Journal. *Marchand. 1913.*

THE PEOPLE'S HOME JOURNAL

Lady Easton's Secret—*A New Novel*—By Lilian Quiller-Couch

15 CENTS INCLUDING A PATTERN   F. M. LUPTON, *Publisher*, NEW YORK   AUGUST · 1922

The People's Home Journal. C.W. Anderson. 1922.

The Country Gentleman. *J. Knowles Hare. 1925.*

The American. *F. Earl Christy. 1924.*

Love. Ertè. c.1920.

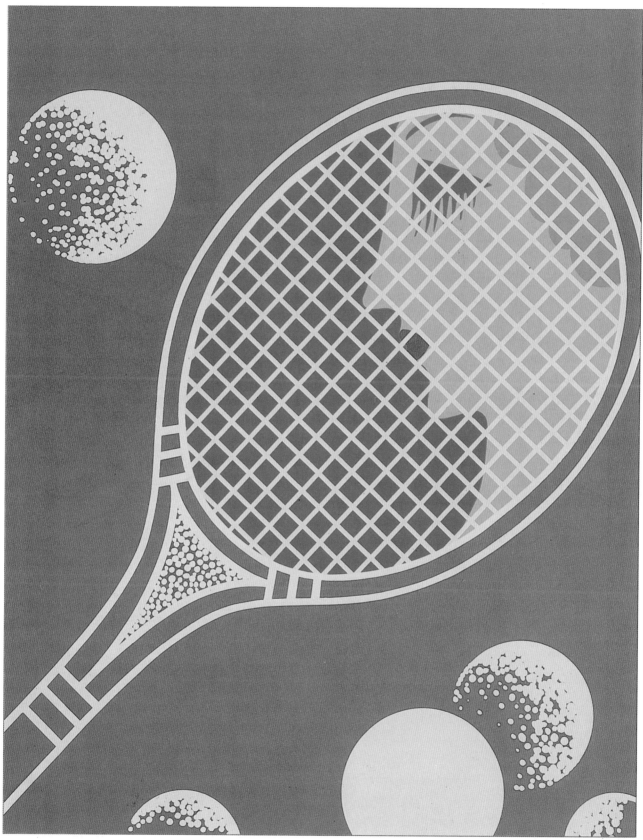

Tennis. Ertè. c.1920.

Vogue. *George Plank. 1921.*

A woman in movement. La Vie Parisienne. Armand Vallée. 1927.

Vogue. *Helen Dryden. 1922.*

Vogue. *Harriet Meserole.* 1920.

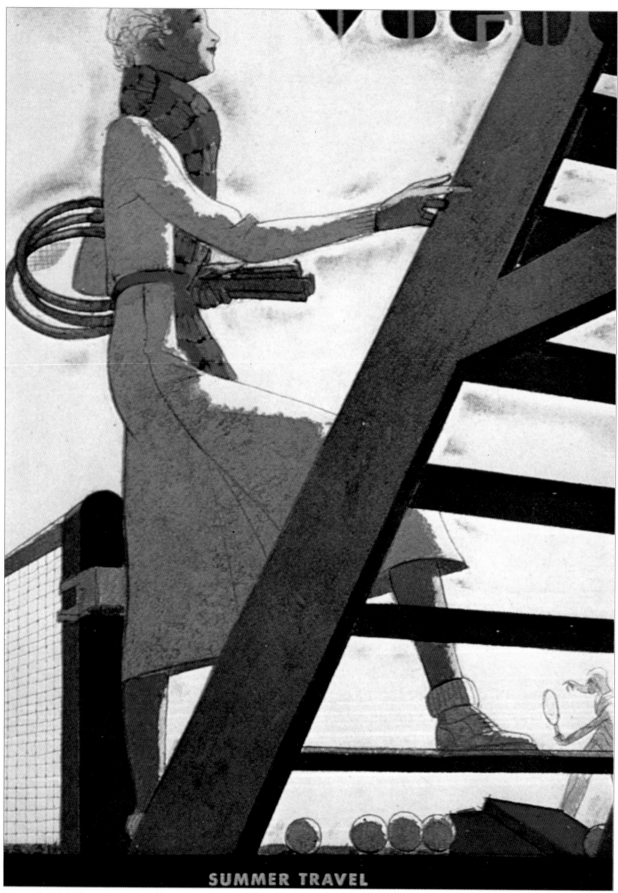

Vogue. Pagès. 1921.

Vogue. *Harriet Meserole. 1927.*

Ladies' Home Journal. *Thomas Webb. 1928.*

The Household Magazine. *Walter Biggs. 1934.*

The American Magazine. *Sheridan. 1932.*

The Country Home. *1930.*

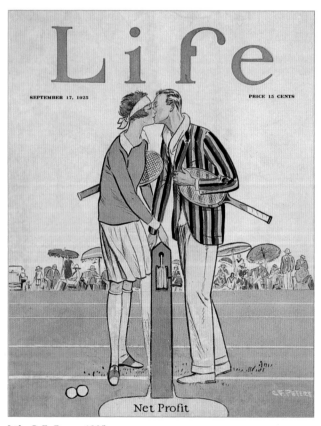

Life. *C.F. Peters. 1925.*

The Saturday Evening Post. *James McKell. 1930.*

The Saturday Evening Post. *Stanlaws. 1934.*

The Saturday Evening Post. *John Lagatta. 1931.*

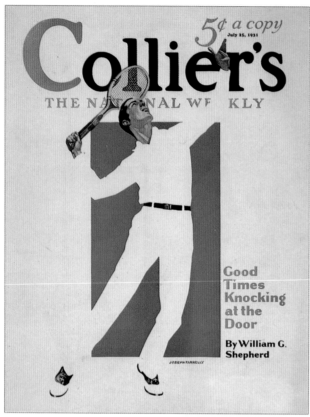

Collier's. *Joseph Farrelly. 1931.*

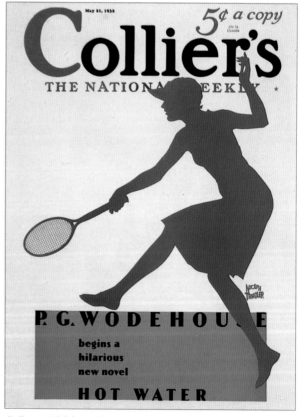

Collier's. *Adolph Treidler. 1932.*

June 1, 1935

5¢ a copy

10c in Canada

Collier's

THE NATIONAL WEEKLY

NRA CODE

H. G. Wells   Quentin Reynolds   "Bugs" Baer

George Creel   Mrs. Lou Gehrig   Peter B. Kyne

© THE CROWELL PUBLISHING COMPANY — PUBLISHERS OF — WOMAN'S HOME COMPANION — THE AMERICAN MAGAZINE — COLLIER'S — THE COUNTRY HOME

Collier's. Gaspano Ricca. 1935.

The Saturday Evening Post. *M.L. Bower. 1936.*

The Saturday Evening Post. *Walt Otto. 1935.*

Liberty. *Mach Tey*. 1933.

Liberty. R. John Holmgren. 1937.

PROFESSIONAL AND LAY

ADVICE ON DRESSING

FOR TENNIS

Left. Though shorts have swept land and sea and now appear, unblushing, even on the courts of Sutton Place, there are still some who just plain don't like them. Hence this chalk-white tennis dress with its dull, clean, slippery texture. Add a scarf after the game and hurl a Scotch cardigan over the shoulders. Best. Bullock's-Wilshire, California.

Right. The Voice of Experience of Helen Jacobs speaking: "Shorts of white serge, because it doesn't wrinkle. A shirt of merino because it absorbs perspiration (Miss Jacobs orders these made and monogrammed by the dozen), socks of cashmere and roll them down low, white duck sneakers from Dunlop Amber-Flash in England. Underneath, wear a satin brassière, nice and slippery when you pull your shirt on top, and B V D underpants of cool white broadcloth. The gabardine jacket is short because with shorts the proportion is better that way." Best.

Right. The best white coat on the horizon, coveted because it is white chinchilla jersey, because it is light, beautifully cut, unornamented by gewgaws, and inexpensive. You couldn't do better if you paid a fortune. The simple white dress is a good one, too. It will come up from the laundry, looking like new. A knitted hat. Bloomingdale's.

54

Vogue. 1934.

SHORTS OR DRESSES THAT LOOK LIKE SHORTS

c.1930.

c.1930.

c.1930.

c.1930.

c.1930.

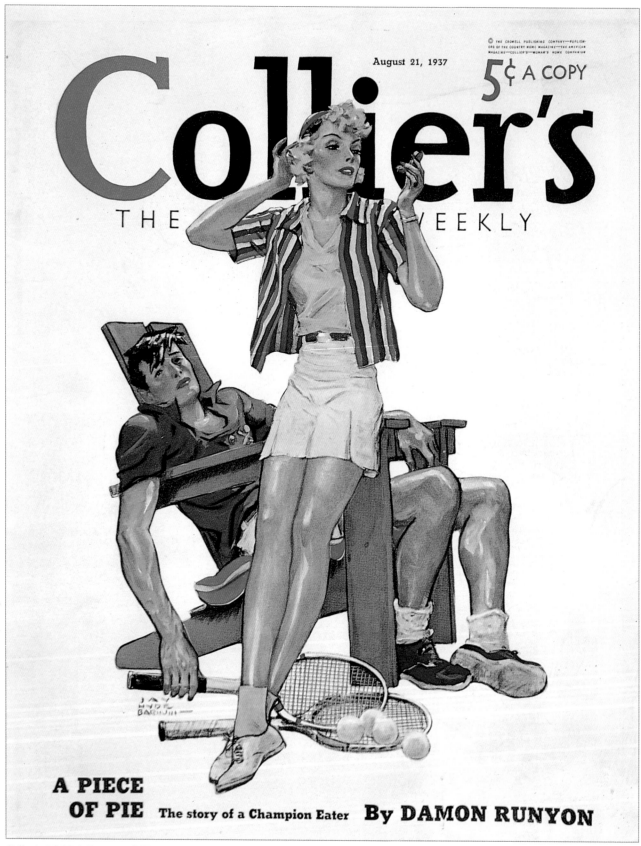

Collier's. *Jay Hyde Barnum. 1937.*

The Saturday Evening Post. *Paul Hesse. 1938.*

ADVERTISING

Liggett and Myers Tobacco Company. Adolph Treidler. 1929

"Advertising is now so near to perfection that it is not easy to propose any improvement."

Samuel Johnson, 1759

*I*n spite of Dr. Johnson's prophesy more than two centuries ago, advertising has indeed seen vast changes and improvements. It has evolved into a major cultural part of our society today, with worldwide advertisers spending over $240 billion a year to promote and sell their goods and services.

Advertising, destined to be the omnipresent, most characteristic and most remunerative form of American literature, did not come into its own until the second half of the nineteenth century.

Prior to the U.S. Civil War, with the factory system still in its infancy, agriculture was the dominant source of national wealth. The market for the products of these early manufacturing and agricultural enterprises was generally the people living in the village, town or city immediately surrounding the producing center.

A fledgling distribution network existed to carry these products to other markets (there were more than 30,000 rail miles in the U.S. in 1860), but there was little demand for its use other than for agricultural products. At this early stage in American manufacturing, sophisticated distribution of goods was not yet developed.

In a selling environment, in which producers were assured of a larger market than their production capacities could meet, it is not surprising to find that most manufacturers did not attempt to differentiate their own products from similar goods. Their products usually carried no identifying brands or marks, and they were normally sold by local retailers from bulk lots, along with the products of other producers.

With the majority of producers thus enjoying an assured market, the small amount of advertising undertaken during this pre-war period was placed by retailers attempting to reach customers in their stores' immediate geographic areas. The medium for carrying these factual-only notices was the local newspaper. Aside from printed notices and posters, this was the only practical choice available.

The U.S. Civil War accelerated a national trend towards industrialization, and for the first time there was some tentative use of advertising beyond the retail level. With the completion of the transcontinental railroad, the continental age of advertising began.

Union Pacific. McClure's Magazine. c.1908.

At the outset of the 1880s manufacturers were blessed by blossoming sales. They had just emerged from a decade that had seen the invention of the telephone, the incandescent lamp and significant innovations in factory products. In 1880 alone there were applications for more than 13,000 copyrights and patents, giving rise to an ever-increasing stream of new products from mills and factories.

The potential consumer markets for these goods were also increasing at a dramatic rate, expanding with the transportation capabilities provided by thousands of miles of railroads and roads throughout the ever-enlarging American nation.

In order to achieve effective distribution of their products, manufacturers needed an advertising medium that could reach all sections of their expanded market area. This medium was the national magazine, transported by the railroad lines into the American towns, where store shelves carried branded products brought by the same rails.

The increasingly popular tool of advertising in magazines led to some spectacular sales successes by its regular users. This success led to a further increase in advertising, which in turn helped to lower the public price of each magazine and, as a result, boosted circulation. Advertisers pumped large sums of money into the industry, as they discovered that the buying power of the rising middle class could best be tapped through magazines. Thus, advertising was inextricably tied to the growth of newspapers, magazines and increased consumerism.

Advertising also changed the entire concept of magazine publishing. Up to this time publishers had generally relied on the readers themselves to pay for the cost of the magazines through the newsstand and subscription prices. But as advertising revenues continued to reward the confidence of advertisers in the medium's ability to economically deliver a selling message, this concept changed. Thus, in 1890 a publisher was quoted as saying, "If I can get a circulation of 400,000, I can afford to give my magazine away to anyone who'll pay the postage." The publisher was no longer simply creating a medium of entertainment, but rather a profitable advertising vehicle that would reach a number of potential customers and fully fund the magazine.

As advanced technology permitted low-cost reproduction of illustrations and color lithography, advertisers became increasingly competitive in their creativity. This led to new found uses of graphics in advertising, in order to give the reader a visual image of the product or to evoke a positive feeling toward the product.

It is not difficult to understand why the English Prime Minister, William Gladstone, insisted on sending to America for magazines, even when English editions were available. It was the American advertisements that fascinated him.

During this period, tennis was associated with a life of leisure, manners and good taste. Advertisers of many products incorporated

The Greenbrier. 1934.

Bill Tilden for Williams Shaving Cream. 1937.

these lifestyle images into their product messages through the use of tennis illustrations. The visual associations consumers made when seeing tennis graphics created increased interest in the sport itself. As the public was hungrily trying new consumer products, they were equally anxious to learn of the exciting and challenging new sport rapidly spreading around the world.

During the 1920s and 1930s advertising art came into its own as never before in history. Greater freedom and larger budgets allowed outstanding artists to use tennis to enrich the appeal of all useful objects. Manufacturers hired some of the best illustrators and artists to create the visual messages they desired.

The illustrations that follow in this volume are wonderful examples of the graphic advances used in advertising during tennis' popular growth years. They invite us to enter a world where one can ward off the ailments of old age and take to the tennis court by using Pabst Extract — "the best tonic," where you flash across the courts with great speed after drinking Canada Dry, or where even when losing, you can show off a winning smile on the court with Colgate dental cream. At the same time they allow us to appreciate how colorful and evocative such a world might be.

P. Lorillard Company. Petty. 1940.

Wright and Ditson. 1888.

Montserrat. 1898.

Elliman and Sons. S.T. Dadd. c.1900.

Postum Cereal Company. 1909.

The Procter and Gamble Company. 1904.

The Coca-Cola Company. 1905.

Kaffee Hag. Ludwig Hohlwein. 1913.

The Strouse-Baer Company. Poucher. 1919.

Cluett, Peabody and Company. 1912.

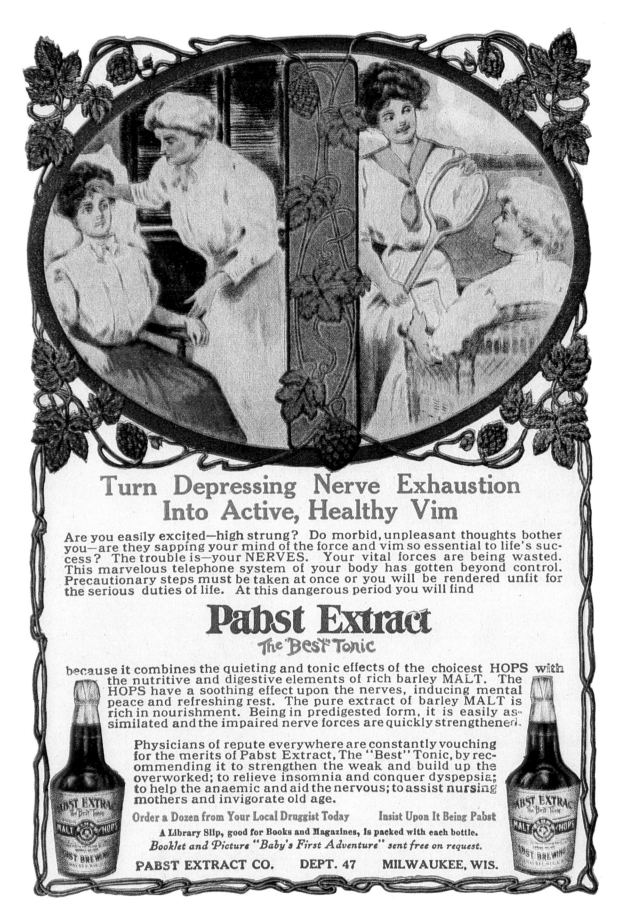

Turn Depressing Nerve Exhaustion Into Active, Healthy Vim

Are you easily excited—high strung? Do morbid, unpleasant thoughts bother you—are they sapping your mind of the force and vim so essential to life's success? The trouble is—your NERVES. Your vital forces are being wasted. This marvelous telephone system of your body has gotten beyond control. Precautionary steps must be taken at once or you will be rendered unfit for the serious duties of life. At this dangerous period you will find

Pabst Extract
The "Best" Tonic

because it combines the quieting and tonic effects of the choicest HOPS with the nutritive and digestive elements of rich barley MALT. The HOPS have a soothing effect upon the nerves, inducing mental peace and refreshing rest. The pure extract of barley MALT is rich in nourishment. Being in predigested form, it is easily assimilated and the impaired nerve forces are quickly strengthened.

Physicians of repute everywhere are constantly vouching for the merits of Pabst Extract, The "Best" Tonic, by recommending it to strengthen the weak and build up the overworked; to relieve insomnia and conquer dyspepsia; to help the anaemic and aid the nervous; to assist nursing mothers and invigorate old age.

Order a Dozen from Your Local Druggist Today   Insist Upon It Being Pabst

A Library Slip, good for Books and Magazines, Is packed with each bottle.
Booklet and Picture "Baby's First Adventure" sent free on request.

PABST EXTRACT CO.   **DEPT. 47**   **MILWAUKEE, WIS.**

Pabst Brewing Company. 1909.

The Procter and Gamble Company. G.A. Beneker. 1917.

H.R. Mallinson and Company. 1920.

Beauty—
safeguard it

Do as all the world is doing—preserve the natural loveliness, which even
sunlight cannot rob of its charm, by following this proved rule in skin care

PALMOLIVE is a beauty soap
made solely for *one* purpose;
to foster good complexions.

In France, home of cosmetics,
Palmolive is the second largest
selling soap, and has supplanted
French soaps by the score. In
beauty-wise Paris, Palmolive is the
"imported" soap.

Remember these facts when
tempted to risk an unproved soap
on your skin.

A BEAUTIFUL complexion lost is hard to
call back again. A beautiful complexion
safeguarded, and made *more* beautiful, is a simple
matter in skin care.

Women all over the world have found that
to be true. The thousands of pretty skins you
see everywhere today overwhelmingly prove the
point. Nature's way is the only true complexion insurance.

Start by ending artificial ways in skin care.
Follow natural ways as foremost skin authorities
urge. The most widely advised skin care of today starts with the *proved rule* below. Just the
simple rule of keeping the pores open, and the
skin gently cleansed every day, with the soothing lather of Palmolive.

Follow this rule for one week—
Note then the changes in your skin

Wash your face gently with soothing
Palmolive Soap, massaging the lather softly into
the skin. Rinse thoroughly, first with warm
water, then with cold. If your skin is inclined
to be dry, apply a touch of good cold cream—
that is all. Do this regularly, and particularly
in the evening. Use powder and rouge if you

wish. But never leave them on over night. They
clog the pores, often enlarge them. Blackheads
and disfigurements often follow. They must
be washed away.

Avoid this mistake

Do not use ordinary soaps in the treatment
given above. Do not think any green soap, or
one represented as of olive and palm oils, is
the same as Palmolive.

And it costs but 10c the cake! So little that
millions let it do for their bodies what it does
for their faces. Obtain a cake today. Then note
what an amazing difference one week makes.

Soap from trees!

The only oils in Palmolive Soap are the
soothing beauty oils from the olive tree, the
African palm, and the coconut palm—and no
other fats whatsoever. That is why Palmolive
Soap is the natural color that it is—for palm
and olive oils, nothing else, give Palmolive its
natural green color.

The only secret to Palmolive is its exclusive
blend—and that is one of the world's priceless
beauty secrets.

THE PALMOLIVE COMPANY (Del. Corp.), CHICAGO, ILLINOIS

*Palmolive Soap is untouched by human hands until
you break the wrapper—it is never sold unwrapped*

Retail
Price 10c

The Colgate-Palmolive Company. 1926.

DISCRIMINATING BUYERS—those who
recognize the value of a good name—appreciate
fully the significance of the emblem, "Body by
Fisher." They know what it guarantees in style,

beauty, comfort and craftsmanship, and in resources that assure a full measure of value. And
because of this, these buyers prefer General
Motors cars—the only cars with Body by Fisher.

CADILLAC · LASALLE · BUICK · OAKLAND · OLDSMOBILE · PONTIAC · CHEVROLET

General Motors. McClelland Barclay. c.1930.

The Coca-Cola Company. c.1920.

Liggett and Myers Tobacco Company. c.1925.

The American Tobacco Company. 1928.

Squibb & Sons. McClelland Barclay. 1926.

The Colgate-Palmolive Company. B. Bistran. 1925.

The Coca-Cola Company. c.1922.

The Andrew Jergens Company. 1926.

Colgate-Palmolive Company. 1925.

Elgin National Watch Company. James Montgomery Flagg. 1925.

Texaco Inc. 1928.

Victorious,,

from Coast to Coast! On every highway, in cars of every type, Texaco Golden Motor Oil—clean and clear—daily demonstrates the flawless, heat-resisting stamina of its finer, sturdier body.

Drive in—wherever you see the Texaco Red Star with the Green T for the *new* and *better* Texaco Gasoline and the full-bodied Texaco Golden Motor Oil.

THE TEXAS COMPANY
TEXACO PETROLEUM PRODUCTS

TEXACO
GOLDEN
MOTOR OIL

FULL BODY

IN ALL GRADES

TEXACO

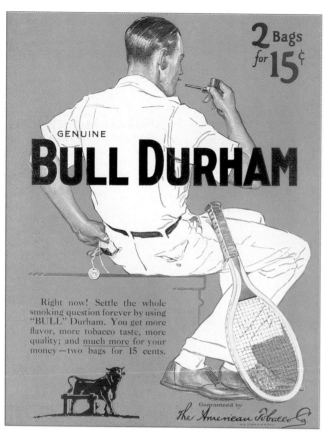

The American Tobacco Company. 1924.

Wilson Brothers Haberdashery. L. Fellows. 1927.

"Well, then, why don't *you* try it too?"

"I like to be original—but do you know why I started using Colgate's? I'll tell you. I was talking to my dentist about toothpastes being good for this and that . . . He said, 'Jean, do you know what a toothpaste is for? A toothpaste is to clean teeth—just that and nothing more.' And he said no toothpaste can do it better than Colgate's. Since I pay my dentist for advice, I'm going to take it. Besides, I like its flavor! And maybe you think the price of a quarter doesn't appeal to me nowadays."

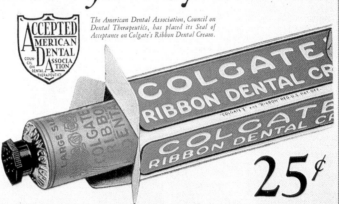

The American Dental Association, Council on Dental Therapeutics, has placed its Seal of Acceptance on Colgate's Ribbon Dental Cream.

The Colgate-Palmolive Company. 1932.

Flashing across the court

At Manheim, Forest Hills, Merion Cricket—
all the famous clubs where championship
tennis is played you'll see "Canada Dry."

Canada Dry. 1930.

ith speed,

their bodies tense as tempered steel!

E a spring unloosed, their bodies snap in smashing serves . . .
racket meets ball in a powerful sweep as they drive shots
the side-line . . . tense at the net they wait and volley in
re-court. . . .

*Keenness and vigor result from drinking this
fine old ginger ale*

are sportsmen . . . lean, sun-tanned, clear-eyed. And here is
portsman's beverage, "Canada Dry." Matching in vigor the
hy bodily activity of countless men and women of this country,
fine ginger ale gives them exhilaration and keenness, more
and delight as they steel themselves for the strenuous play
e them. It is a delightfully refreshing beverage after exercise!

*Careful methods of making assure an unmatched
excellence of flavor*

onder! This fine old ginger ale has excellence—the quality of
smen. Its very foundation is "Liquid Ginger"—which we
from selected Jamaica ginger root by a special process. This
ss is exclusively controlled by us and, unlike any other
od, retains for "Canada Dry" all of the original aroma, flavor
natural essence of the ginger root. Rigid laboratory control
es uniformity, purity and highest quality. A special process
rbonation enables "Canada Dry" to retain its sparkle long
the bottle has been opened. Taste it and notice the difference.
der such careful methods of making, this fine old ginger ale

*Here is the convenient Hostess Package of 12 bottles. There's a place in
your pantry for it over the holiday; or a place in your car if you go on a
picnic or a motor trip.*

has quite rightly won the approving nod of
connoisseurs the wide world over. In great
hotels and clubs . . . on transatlantic liners
. . . in London, Paris, New York . . . in
many, many homes throughout this country.

Serve it in your home. At dinner, at
luncheon, its marvelous flavor adds new
delight to a meal. In the Hostess Package
of 12 bottles "Canada Dry" will always
be conveniently on hand. Order it soon!

"CANADA DRY"
Reg. U. S. Pat. Off.

The Champagne of Ginger Ales

The Clicquot Club Company. c.1935.

Canada Dry. 1934.

Canada Dry. 1937.

a farewell to thirst

ACROSS the Country Club bar . . . at the roadside barbecue . . . over the ice-box back home . . . wherever thirsts are to be quenched . . . there you will hear demands for Orange-Crush—the natural *fresh* orange beverage . . . Made from the rich, fresh juices of the whole orange, including the tangy flavor of the golden peel, sweetened with pure cane sugar, sparkling with carbonated water . . . Orange-Crush is praised everywhere for its delicious flavor. No after-thirst . . . No other orange drink is Orange-Crush. So to make sure you get it, be sure you say *one word more*—say Orange-CRUSH. On sale wherever thirst is quenched. In the *krinkly* bottle or at all the better fountains

▼

Other Fresh Fruit Drinks—Lime-Crush from fresh limes—Grape-Crush from fresh grapes—Cocoa-Crush from fresh-roasted cocoa beans

Say **Orange -Crush**

TRADE MARK REG. U.S. PAT OFF.

MADE FROM *fresh* ORANGES

Orange Crush. 1931.

July

Like so many other things in this modern world, tennis isn't what it was and it would seem unlikely, therefore, that Bluff King Hal would approve of Wimbledon. It may, perhaps, console this much-married monarch to know that nowadays we call *his* game 'Royal Tennis' and some of us still play it. But, from the game which, literally, was the sport of kings in the 16th and 17th centuries, we have evolved our own version and Tennis has (in the current idiom) been democratised. Now, that is a Good Thing; and the same process can be seen at work in other directions. Banking—although never exactly a sport of kings—was certainly at one time a privilege of wealth. It is quite otherwise today, when thousands of people of all occupations and all walks of life regard it as normal and unexceptional that they should possess accounts at the Midland Bank. And that is a Very Good Thing Indeed.

MIDLAND BANK LIMITED

2,150 branches in England and Wales

HEAD OFFICE, POULTRY, LONDON, E.C.2

Midland Bank Limited. [illustration from 16th c.] 1958.

POSTCARDS

HAVING A FINE TIME

England. c.1910.

HISTORY OF THE PICTURE POSTCARD

"When archaeologists of the thirtieth century begin to excavate...ruins..., they will focus their attention on the picture postcard as the best means of penetrating the spirit of the...era. They will collect and collate thousands of these cards and they will reconstruct our epoque from the strange hieroglyphics and images they reveal, spared by the passage of time."

James Douglas English journalist, 1907

Belgium. 1925

𝒫icture postcards originated in Europe in the early 1870s. Production increased in the 1890s with the introduction of new printing techniques and the extension of licenses to private industry to publish postcards. Collotype printing became available on an industrial scale, which led to a proliferation of photographic postcards and color lithography.

Social and cultural factors encouraged the growth of postcards well into the twentieth century. The brevity of the verbal message and the presence of the illustration to augment the written word, by amplifying its meaning or charging it with allusions, were among the reasons for the extraordinary popularity of postcards.

The appearance of the postcard brought about some interesting changes in Victorian and Edwardian letter-writing habits. A letter's contents were concealed inside an envelope, which was considered an improper means of communication for young lovers. A postcard, on the other hand, made it possible to inspect what was written and was therefore more acceptable.

"Like many great inventions," observed the English journalist James Douglas in 1907, "the postcard has brought a silent revolution in our habits. It has freed us unexpectedly from the fatigue of writing letters. There is no space for courtesy."

The postcard became a means of picturesque documentation at a low price, and it was coveted by millions of collectors worldwide. Postcards served as a substitute for those who could not afford first-hand experiences of the places and the subjects represented in them. At the turn of the century, postcard stalls or kiosks were a common sight in public gardens and exhibition parks in European cities, as were postcard salesmen passing along trains, or from table to table in cafes and restaurants.

Before 1907 writing was generally not permitted on the address and stamp side of the postcard (the reverse side of the graphic). Senders of cards had to write their message over the image on the front (graphic) side. In 1907 it became permissible for the writer to use the newly created divided back side for the message, keeping the graphic image clean for the recipient and for posterity.

The golden age of the picture postcard ran from 1898 to the end of the World War I in 1918. During those twenty years many artists and photographers in Europe, the United States and elsewhere developed graphics for postcard publishers. The postcard brought both art and the photographic experience within the range of the general public.

Women assumed a central role in postcard iconography, and they were popularized by postcard artists in many different situations. Artists often escaped into fantasy with their symbolic and sublime elevations of women into stylized, idealized beings. Significantly, the woman was the principal subject in most illustrators' work, even when there was a man at her side.

Children also figured prominently in picture postcards throughout the world. In most cases, the image of childhood, with its uninhibited joy in living, its implicit message of hope for the future, and its innocence and openness, was bound up with such messages or greetings as: "Happy Christmas," "Happy Easter" and "Happy New Year."

Sport in general, including tennis, has always been a major theme of picture postcards. Participatory sport emerged as a new phenomenon around the turn of the century, its mass appeal becoming synonymous with modernism. Sport was a heroic activity, and tennis became an intensely popular postcard subject worldwide.

The postcard was also a means of promoting or reflecting trends in current fashion. As such, postcards are valuable records of tennis fashions for both men and women throughout the historic period covered in this volume.

With the availability of photographic postcards, tennis photos became a popular subject for many postcard publishers, bringing the view closer to the beauty on the courts. Many tennis clubs, recognizing the benefits of worldwide attention and publicity, published their own picture postcards to promote their tourist facilities and to further the glamorous appeal of the sport.

Postcards became important documents for revealing the international spread of tennis as a popular sport. Without the availability of this medium, much of the populace would have had no resource for discovering the excitement of tennis.

While collections of postcards in public museums do exist today, the collection of cards is primarily the domain of individuals who buy and trade cards, much as their grandparents did generations ago. Now many collectors also do so to preserve and record history.

France. c.1925.

When viewed closely, each postcard in this collection has a story to tell. The scenery, characters and action scenes are static, but they can be brought to life vividly with a bit of imagination and with close attention to the depictions of clothing styles, tennis equipment and locations. Through close observation these images can greatly enhance our ability to imagine the experience of tennis as it existed around the turn of the century.

Belgium. F. Toussaint. c.1899.

Germany. B. Wennerberg. c.1900.

England. 1905.

England. c.1908.

Europe. 1908.

Europe. 1906.

Europe. 1908.

MISS MARIE STUDHOLME

England. c.1910.

Europe. 1909.

Europe. c.1910.

France. 1909.

USA. 1911.

The game's the thing; oh, lovely girl,
    Graceful, lithe as fleeting doe,
The out-of-door and you are one,
    Your cheeks a very sunlight glow.

USA. 1905.

LOVE'S FIRST TOKEN.

USA. 1909.

USA. 1911.

USA. 1911.

Germany. 1906.

USA. 1911.

France. c.1910

Belgium. 1915.

Germany. 1906.

Germany. c.1910.

Germany. c.1910.

England. c.1910.

England. 1915.

France. c.1915.

USA. 1907.

France. H. Eliot. c.1900.

England. 1908.

England. 1908.

THE TENNIS GIRL
She likes to court in the court,
Thinks tennis "the jolliest sport!"
And shouts "thirty all!"
As she whacks at the ball
With many a cowlike cavort!

USA. 1906.

PEOPLE WHO SAY TENNIS IS SLOW
EVIDENTLY DON'T KNOW THE FINER
POINTS OF THE GAME!

USA. c.1910.

England. c.1915.

USA. c.1910.

USA. 1910.

USA. 1907.

Je vois dans votre doux sourire
Mille promesses de bonheur;
Dans vos yeux brillants je vois luire
Tout ce que pense votre cœur.

France. 1909.

IT'S ALL LOVE

698/

USA. c.1915.

HE: " Will you be my partner?"
SHE: "Oh! this is so sudden!"

USA. 1910.

USA. Farina. 1907.

England. Luis Usabal. c.1910.

England. 1916.

Belgium. 1919.

USA. 1912.

Germany. Paul Fischer. 1912.

USA. 1908.

France. 1913.

France. 1913.

USA. F. Earl Christy. 1913.

USA. F. Earl Christy. c.1915.

"LOVE"

USA. 1910.

USA. S. Norman. 1913.

Europe. Luis Usabal. c.1920.

Europe. Luis Usabal. 1920.

"The Tennis Girl."

England. c.1915.

France. Xavier Sager. c.1910.

England. c.1915.

England. c.1938.

England. c.1915.

Paris. c.1915.

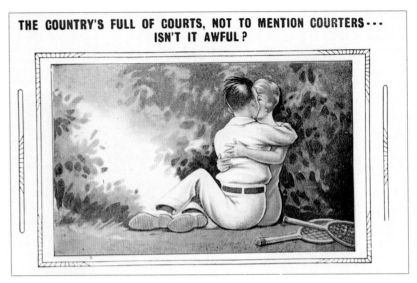

USA. c.1910.

USA. c.1910.

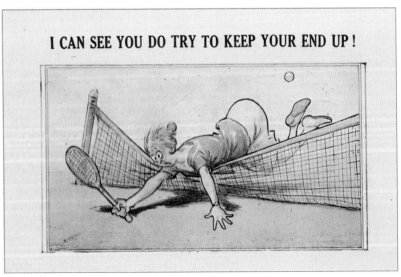

USA. c.1910.

Europe. c.1915.

Europe. c.1915.

Europe. c.1915.

Belgium. André Marty. c.1920.

Czechoslavakia. c.1935.

Germany. 1909.

Italy. 1940.

England. c.1920.

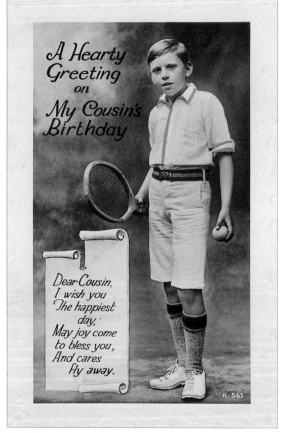

England. c.1920.

France. c.1925.

France. 1927.

France. 1924.

France. 1932.

France. c.1920.

England. 1918.

THE ART OF TENNIS

France. c.1920.

France. c.1920.

France. c.1920.

France. c.1920.

USA. 1926.

England. c.1925.

LE JEU DE L'AMOUR.

France. 1933.

L'AMOUR DU JEU.

France. 1933.

USA. 1912.

USA. c.1920.

USA. c.1920.

USA. c.1920.

England. 1930.

France. c.1920.

France. c.1920.

France. c.1920.

England. c.1920.

Germany. c.1925.

USA. c.1930.

USA. c.1930.

France. 1925.

France. 1925.

France. 1925.

France. 1925.

Belgium. 1925.

France. c.1920.

ACKNOWLEDGEMENTS

Nearly all of the artwork and graphic materials reproduced in this book are from the personal collection of the author. Ownership of and permission to use these and other materials reproduced herein are acknowledged below. While the publisher makes every effort possible to publish full and correct information for every work, in some cases errors may occur. The publisher regrets any such errors but must disclaim any liability in this regard.

American Tobacco Company

Arrow Shirts. Reprinted with permission of Cluett, Peabody & Co., Inc.,
    manufacturer of Arrow Shirts.

Canada Dry. Cadbury Schweppes Inc.

Chesterfield. Liggett Group Incorporated.

Clicquot Club Ginger Ale. Cott Beverages Limited.

Coca-Cola. Coca-Cola is a registered trademark of The Coca-Cola Company and
    is used with permission.

Colgate, Palmolive and Wildroot Taroleum Hair Wash. Colgate-Palmolive
    Company.

Country Gentleman. Copyright © Curtis Publishing Co. Reprinted by permission.

Elgin Watch Company. Elgin National Industries, Incorporated.

General Motors. Reprinted with permission of General Motors Corporation.

Ivory Soap. Courtesy of Procter & Gamble. Reproduced with permission.

Jergens. Andrew Jergens Company.

Ladies' Home Journal. © Copyright 1928, Meridith Corporation. All rights
    reserved. Reprinted from *Ladies' Home Journal* magazine.

Mallinson's Silks de Luxe. Burlington Industries, Inc.

Midland Bank. Reproduced by kind permission of Midland Bank PLC.

Pabst Brewing Company.

Saturday Evening Post. Copyright © Curtis Publishing Company. Reprinted by
    permission.

Squibbs Dental Cream. © Copyright 1926, E.R. Squibb & Sons, Inc. Reprinted
    by permission of copyright owner.

Texaco. Texaco Inc.

Union Pacific Railroad.

White Sulpher Springs. The Greenbrier.

Williams Shaving Cream. Reprinted with permission of Smithkline Beecham
    Consumer Brands.

INDEX